Computerised Accounting Practice Set
Using Sage One Online Accounting

Expert Level

This expert level computerised accounting practice set is for students who need to practice exercises of Sage One Online Accounting, students can record a month's transactions of Richmond Papers Pty Ltd and can create financial reports.

It covers the following topics.

- Setting Up a New Accounting System
- Suppliers, Purchases and Inventory
- Customers, Sales and Inventory
- Receipts, Payments and Expenses
- Bank Reconciliation
- Financial Reports

Syed Tirmizi
Certified Advisor

ISBN 978-0-9945988-3-7

9 780994 598837 >

For enquiries, please contact **syed.tirmizi@mail.com**

Part A
Practice Set

This page is blank.

Instructions

You have recently been appointed as an Accounts Assistant at Richmond Papers Pty Ltd, a new business dealing in printing and publishing. Your responsibilities are to set up a computerised accounting system, update the company records and produce financial reports.

The company started trading on 1st April 2016. All documents have been checked for accuracy and owner of the business, John Smith has authorised these documents.

The company uses straight line method for depreciating its non-current assets at 10% yearly. The policy defines the decline in value of these non-current assets on monthly basis.

You are required to complete the following tasks for April 2016 in the order given.

a) Setting Up a New Accounting System
b) Suppliers, Purchases and Inventory
c) Customers, Sales and Inventory
d) Receipts, Payments and Expenses
e) Bank Reconciliation
f) Financial Reports

a) Setting Up a New Accounting System

Create a new company in Sage One Online Accounting using the following information.

Company Name	Richmond Papers Pty Ltd
ABN	46 995 263 632
Address	23 High Street
	Richmond
	VIC 3121
Phone Number	03 9988 7766
Current Financial Year	Jul 2015 – Jun 2016

Set up Suppliers, Customers and Items with the help of Tables 1, 2 and 3.

Additional Information

i. On April 1st 2016, $25,000 Capital was introduced by the owner of the business and was paid into the Bank Current Account. The reference for this transaction is CR0001.
ii. On April 2nd 2016, the Company purchased a motor vehicle from Western Motors for $12,000 + $1,200 GST. Cheque number 000001 was used to make the settlement.
iii. At the end of the month depreciation on the motor vehicle and bank service charges are to be recorded to the relevant accounts.

Table 1: Suppliers

Supplier Account Details	
Mark & Tony 41 Middlesbrough Road St Albans - VIC 3021 Credit Limit: $3,000 ABN: 84 678 592 583	Contact Name: Sue Hawkins Email: sales@mt.com.au Telephone: 03 9876 5432 Default Tax Type: GST Payment Terms: 30 days from the date of invoice
David & Sons 67 Longwood Road Craigieburn - VIC 3064 Credit Limit: $15,000 ABN: 65 473 985 624	Contact Name: John Alexander Email: sales@ds.com.au Telephone: 03 9765 4321 Default Tax Type: GST Payment Terms: 30 days from the date of invoice
Ian & Co Pty Ltd 94 High Street Fitzroy - VIC 3065 Credit Limit: $5,000 ABN: 25 657 917 634	Contact Name: Angela Samson Email: sales@ic.com.au Telephone: 03 9654 3210 Default Tax Type: GST Payment Terms: 30 days from the date of invoice
Smith & Baker 11 Westfield Road Lalor - VIC 3075 Credit Limit: $3,000 ABN: 54 637 945 746	Contact Name: Andrew Smith Email: sales@sb.com.au Telephone: 03 9543 2109 Default Tax Type: GST Payment Terms: 30 days from the date of invoice
Gary Corporation 94 Wellington Street Preston - VIC 3072 Credit Limit: $5,000 ABN: 74 325 496 324	Contact Name: Adam Miller Email: sales@gc.com.au Telephone: 03 9432 1098 Default Tax Type: GST Payment Terms: 30 days from the date of invoice
East End Pty Ltd 34 Canterbury Road Epping - VIC 3076 Credit Limit: $5,000 ABN: 96 376 843 587	Contact Name: Nick Abbey Email: sales@ee.com.au Telephone: 03 9321 0987 Default Tax Type: GST Payment Terms: 30 days from the date of invoice

Table 2: Customers

Customer Account Details	
Peter Electronics 9 Western Avenue Brooklyn - VIC 3012 Credit Limit: $3,000 ABN: 52 639 846 324	Contact Name: Megan Boucher Email: info@pe.com.au Telephone: 03 9123 4567 Default Tax Type: GST Payment Terms: 30 days from the date of invoice
Western Estate Agents 362 High Street Sunshine - VIC 3029 Credit Limit: $2,000 ABN: 47 528 963 764	Contact Name: Ashley Champ Email: info@wea.com.au Telephone: 03 9234 5678 Default Tax Type: GST Payment Terms: 30 days from the date of invoice
Surf Stores 54 Dundee Street Deer Park - VIC 3023 Credit Limit: $3,000 ABN: 95 768 359 862	Contact Name: Natalie Dunn Email: info@ss.com.au Telephone: 03 9345 6789 Default Tax Type: GST Payment Terms: 30 days from the date of invoice
Sally's Warehouse 12 Wood Street Essendon - VIC 3040 Credit Limit: $10,000 ABN: 76 662 485 964	Contact Name: George Gordon Email: info@sw.com.au Telephone: 03 9456 7890 Default Tax Type: GST Payment Terms: 30 days from the date of invoice
Horizon Designs 32 Abbots Road Broadmeadows - VIC 3047 Credit Limit: $6,000 ABN: 12 528 972 562	Contact Name: Lee Hopkins Email: info@hd.com.au Telephone: 03 9567 8901 Default Tax Type: GST Payment Terms: 30 days from the date of invoice
Thomson Clothings 84 Spring Street Thomastown - VIC 3074 Credit Limit: $5,000 ABN: 74 635 842 321	Contact Name: Alston Leeson Email: info@thc.com.au Telephone: 03 9678 9012 Default Tax Type: GST Payment Terms: 30 days from the date of invoice
Globe Travels Pty Ltd 42 Barry Road Melbourne - VIC 3000 Credit Limit: $10,000 ABN: 85 365 412 741	Contact Name: Robert Nickelson Email: info@gt.com.au Telephone: 03 9789 0123 Default Tax Type: GST Payment Terms: 30 days from the date of invoice
Tiffany Cakes 36 High Road Williamstown - VIC 3016 Credit Limit: $10,000 ABN: 78 635 254 524	Contact Name: Anthony Robins Email: info@tc.com.au Telephone: 03 9890 1234 Default Tax Type: GST Payment Terms: 30 days from the date of invoice

Table 3: Items

Items Details	
Item Code: A3CP Description: A3 Copy Paper Inclusive Selling Price: $40 Unit: Each	Sales Account: A3 Copy Paper Purchases Account: A3 Copy Paper Tax on Sales: GST Tax on Purchases: GST
Item Code: A4CP Description: A4 Copy Paper Inclusive Selling Price: $15 Unit: Each	Sales Account: A4 Copy Paper Purchases Account: A4 Copy Paper Tax on Sales: GST Tax on Purchases: GST
Item Code: A5CP Description: A5 Copy Paper Inclusive Selling Price: $14 Unit: Each	Sales Account: A5 Copy Paper Purchases Account: A5 Copy Paper Tax on Sales: GST Tax on Purchases: GST
Item Code: COLO Description: Coloured Paper Inclusive Selling Price: $20 Unit: Each	Sales Account: Coloured Paper Purchases Account: Coloured Paper Tax on Sales: GST Tax on Purchases: GST
Item Code: EN01 Description: Envelopes Large Inclusive Selling Price: $35 Unit: Each	Sales Account: Envelopes Large Purchases Account: Envelopes Large Tax on Sales: GST Tax on Purchases: GST
Item Code: RR18 Description: Register Rolls Inclusive Selling Price: $54 Unit: Each	Sales Account: Register Rolls Purchases Account: Register Rolls Tax on Sales: GST Tax on Purchases: GST

b) Suppliers, Purchases and Inventory

Enter the following purchase invoices and purchase returns into the computer.

Purchase Invoices

Date	Supplier	Supp. Inv.	Item	Description	Qty	Cost	Gross Amt Inc GST
April 2nd	Gary Corporation	412	A3CP	A3 Copy Paper	200	$25.00	$5,000.00
April 2nd	Smith & Baker	G/749	A5CP	A5 Copy Paper	250	$8.00	$2,000.00
April 4th	Ian & Co. Pty Ltd	00854	A4CP	A4 Copy Paper	500	$8.00	$4,000.00
April 5th	David & Sons	2016-18	RR18	Register Rolls	350	$38.00	$13,300.00
April 7th	Mark & Tony	A423	COLO	Coloured Paper	200	$14.00	$2,800.00
April 9th	East End Pty Ltd	EE2141	EN01	Envelopes Large	200	$22.00	$4,400.00

Purchase Returns

Date	Supplier	Supp. Inv.	Item	Description	Qty	Cost	Gross Amt Inc GST
April 4th	Smith & Baker	G/749	A5CP	A5 Copy Paper	20	$8.00	$160.00
April 11th	David & Sons	2016-18	RR18	Register Rolls	25	$38.00	$950.00

c) Customers, Sales and Inventory

Enter the following sales invoices and sales returns into the computer.

Sales Invoices

Date	Customer	Doc. No.	Item	Description	Qty	Price	Amount Inc GST
April 5th	Horizon Designs	001	A4CP	A4 Copy Paper	70	$14.50	$1,015.00
			RR18	Register Rolls	60	$54.00	$3,240.00
			A5CP	A5 Copy Paper	70	$14.00	$980.00
						Total	$5,235.00
April 10th	Thomson Clothings	002	A4CP	A4 Copy Paper	60	$15.00	$900.00
			EN01	Envelopes Large	80	$35.00	$2,800.00
						Total	$3,700.00
April 12th	Globe Travels Pty Ltd	003	A4CP	A4 Copy Paper	60	$15.00	$900.00
			A3CP	A3 Copy Paper	50	$40.00	$2,000.00
			RR18	Register Rolls	70	$54.00	$3,780.00
			COLO	Coloured Paper	60	$20.00	$1,200.00
						Total	$7,880.00
April 14th	Tiffany Cakes	004	A4CP	A4 Copy Paper	50	$15.00	$750.00
			RR18	Register Rolls	60	$54.00	$3,240.00
			EN01	Envelopes Large	60	$35.00	$2,100.00
						Total	$6,090.00
April 19th	Peter Electronics	005	A4CP	A4 Copy Paper	60	$15.00	$900.00
			COLO	Coloured Paper	70	$20.00	$1,400.00
						Total	$2,300.00
April 21st	Sally's Warehouse	006	A4CP	A4 Copy Paper	70	$15.00	$1,050.00
			COLO	Coloured Paper	60	$20.00	$1,200.00
			A3CP	A3 Copy Paper	70	$40.00	$2,800.00
			RR18	Register Rolls	50	$54.00	$2,700.00
						Total	$7,750.00
April 25th	Western Estate Agents	007	A5CP	A5 Copy Paper	100	$14.00	$1,400.00
						Total	$1,400.00
April 27th	Surf Stores	008	A4CP	A4 Copy Paper	50	$15.00	$750.00
			RR18	Register Rolls	30	$54.00	$1,620.00
						Total	$2,370.00

Sales Returns

Date	Customer	Doc. No.	Item	Description	Qty	Price	Amount Inc GST
April 17th	Thomson Clothings	002	EN01	Envelopes Large	20	$35.00	$700.00
April 23rd	Sally's Warehouse	006	A4CP	A4 Copy Paper	10	$15.00	$150.00

d) Receipts, Payments and Expenses

Enter the following payments received from customers, payments made to suppliers and expenses into the computer.

Payments Received

Date	Receipt Type	Customer	Details	Amount ($)
April 13th	EFT	Horizon Designs	Invoice 001	$5,235.00
April 18th	Cheque	Thomson Clothings	Invoice 002	$3,000.00
April 20th	Cheque	Globe Travels Ltd	Invoice 003	$7,880.00
April 25th	EFT	Tiffany Cakes	Invoice 004	$6,090.00

Expenses Summary

Date	Cheque No.	Expenses	Details	Net	Tax	Gross ($)
April 2nd	000002	Rent	Richmond Real Estate	$1,000.00	$100.00	$1,100.00
April 7th	000003	Insurance Premium	Melbourne Insurance	$200.00	$20.00	$220.00
April 19th	000004	Electricity Bill	Victoria Electricity	$176.73	$17.67	$194.40
April 21st	000005	Telephone Bill	Australia Telecom	$196.92	$19.62	$215.84
April 26th	000006	Cleaning	Melbourne Removals	$50.00	$5.00	$55.00

Payments Made

Date	Cheque No.	Supplier	Details	Amount ($)
April 28th	000007	Gary Corporation	412	$5,000.00
April 28th	000008	Smith & Baker	G/749	$1,840.00

e) Bank Reconciliation

Prepare bank reconciliation for the month of April 2016. Company bank statement is as follows.

BANK OF RICHMOND

36 Spring Street, Richmond, VIC 3121   **Cheque Account Statement**

TEL 1800 AUSTRALIA   30-04-2016

Richmond Papers Pty Ltd

23 High Street

Richmond

VIC 3121

	BSB Number	Account Number
	123-456	987654321

Date	Details	Ref	Withdrawal	Deposits	Balance
01-Apr-16	Account opened - Initial deposit			$25,000.00	$25,000.00
02-Apr-16	CHQ 000001		$13,200.00		$11,800.00
02-Apr-16	CHQ 000002		$1,100.00		$10,700.00
07-Apr-16	CHQ 000003		$220.00		$10,480.00
13-Apr-16	EFT – Horizon Designs			$5,235.00	$15,715.00
18-Apr-16	Cheque deposited			$3,000.00	$18,715.00
19-Apr-16	CHQ 000004		$194.40		$18,520.60
20-Apr-16	Cheque deposited			$7,880.00	$26,400.60
21-Apr-16	CHQ 000005		$215.84		$26,184.76
22-Apr-16	CHQ 000007		$5,000.00		$21,184.76
25-Apr-16	EFT – Tiffany Cakes			$6,090.00	$27,274.76
30-Apr-16	Bank charges		$10.00		$27,264.76
Totals			**$19,930.24**	**$47,205.00**	

f) Financial Reports

Print or save the following reports for the month of April 2016.

I.   Supplier Listing Report Detailed
II.   Supplier Transactions Report
III.   Customer Listing Report Detailed
IV.   Customer Transactions Report
V.   Purchases By Item Report
VI.   Item Valuation Report
VII.   Banks and Credit Cards Transactions Report
VIII. Bank Reconciliation Report
IX.   Journal Entries Report
X.   Trial Balance Report
XI.   Profit and Loss Report
XII.   Balance Sheet Report

Part B

Solutions

This page is blank.

Supplier Listing Report

Richmond Papers Pty Ltd

Date: 09/05/2016
Page: 1/1

Name	Category		Active	Contact Name	Telephone	Balance
David & Sons			Yes	John Alexander	0397654321	$12,350.00
Physical Address:	**Postal Address:**	**Fax:**				
67 Longwood Road	67 Longwood Road	**Mobile:**				
Craigieburn	Craigieburn	**Email:**		sales@ds.com.au		
VIC	VIC	**Credit Limit:**		$15,000.00		
3064	3064					
East End Pty Ltd			Yes	Nick Abbey	0393210987	$4,400.00
Physical Address:	**Postal Address:**	**Fax:**				
34 Canterbury Road	34 Canterbury Road	**Mobile:**				
Epping	Epping	**Email:**		sales@ee.com.au		
VIC	VIC	**Credit Limit:**		$5,000.00		
3076	3076					
Gary Corporation			Yes	Adam Miller	0394321098	$0.00
Physical Address:	**Postal Address:**	**Fax:**				
94 Wellington Street	94 Wellington Street	**Mobile:**				
Preston	Preston	**Email:**		sales@gc.com.au		
VIC	VIC	**Credit Limit:**		$5,000.00		
3072	3072					
Ian & Co Pty Ltd			Yes	Angela Samson	0396543210	$4,000.00
Physical Address:	**Postal Address:**	**Fax:**				
94 High Street	94 High Street	**Mobile:**				
Fitzroy	Fitzroy	**Email:**		sales@ic.com.au		
VIC	VIC	**Credit Limit:**		$5,000.00		
3065	3065					
Mark & Tony			Yes	Sue Hawkins	0398765432	$2,800.00
Physical Address:	**Postal Address:**	**Fax:**				
41 Middlesbrough Road	41 Middlesbrough Road	**Mobile:**				
St Albans	St Albans	**Email:**		sales@mt.com.au		
VIC	VIC	**Credit Limit:**		$3,000.00		
3021	3021					
Smith & Baker			Yes	Andrew Smith	0395432109	$0.00
Physical Address:	**Postal Address:**	**Fax:**				
11 Westfield Road	11 Westfield Road	**Mobile:**				
Lalor	Lalor	**Email:**		sales@sb.com.au		
VIC	VIC	**Credit Limit:**		$3,000.00		
3075	3075					

Supplier Transactions Report

Richmond Papers Pty Ltd

Supplier: All Suppliers
Category: All Categories
Date Range: 01/04/2016 - 30/04/2016

Supplier Date	Reference	Transaction Type	Description	Debit	Credit	Balance
David & Sons						
Opening Balance as at: 01/04/2016					$ 0.00	
05/04/2016 SIV0000004		Supplier Invoice	2016-18		$ 13,300.00	$ 13,300.00
22/04/2016 RTN0000002		Supplier Return	2016-18	$ 950.00		$ 12,350.00
Closing Balance as at: 30/04/2016					$ 12,350.00	
Movement for the period					$ 12,350.00	
East End Pty Ltd						
Opening Balance as at: 01/04/2016					$ 0.00	
09/04/2016 SIV0000006		Supplier Invoice	EE2141		$ 4,400.00	$ 4,400.00
Closing Balance as at: 30/04/2016					$ 4,400.00	
Movement for the period					$ 4,400.00	
Gary Corporation						
Opening Balance as at: 01/04/2016					$ 0.00	
02/04/2016 SIV0000001		Supplier Invoice	412		$ 5,000.00	$ 5,000.00
22/04/2016 PAY0000001		Supplier Payment	000007	$ 5,000.00		$ 0.00
Closing Balance as at: 30/04/2016					$ 0.00	
Movement for the period					$ 0.00	
Ian & Co Pty Ltd						
Opening Balance as at: 01/04/2016					$ 0.00	
04/04/2016 SIV0000003		Supplier Invoice	00854		$ 4,000.00	$ 4,000.00
Closing Balance as at: 30/04/2016					$ 4,000.00	
Movement for the period					$ 4,000.00	
Mark & Tony						
Opening Balance as at: 01/04/2016					$ 0.00	
07/04/2016 SIV0000005		Supplier Invoice	A423		$ 2,800.00	$ 2,800.00
Closing Balance as at: 30/04/2016					$ 2,800.00	
Movement for the period					$ 2,800.00	
Smith & Baker						
Opening Balance as at: 01/04/2016					$ 0.00	
02/04/2016 SIV0000002		Supplier Invoice	G/749		$ 2,000.00	$ 2,000.00
22/04/2016 RTN0000001		Supplier Return	G/749	$ 160.00		$ 1,840.00
28/04/2016 PAY0000002		Supplier Payment	000008	$ 1,840.00		$ 0.00
Closing Balance as at: 30/04/2016					$ 0.00	
Movement for the period					$ 0.00	
Grand Total:					$ 23,550.00	

Customer Listing Report

Richmond Papers Pty Ltd

Date: 09/05/2016
Page: 1/2

Name	Category	Active	Contact Name	Telephone	Balance
Globe Travels Pty Ltd		Yes	Robert Nickelson	0397890123	$0.00

Delivery Address:	**Postal Address:**	**Fax:**		
42 Barry Road	42 Barry Road	**Mobile:**		
Melbourne	Melbourne	**Email:**	info@gt.com.au	
VIC	VIC	**Credit Limit:**	$10,000.00	
		Sales Rep:		
3000	3000	**Default Price List:**	Default Price List	

Name	Category	Active	Contact Name	Telephone	Balance
Horizon Designs		Yes	Lee Hopkins	0395678901	$0.00

Delivery Address:	**Postal Address:**	**Fax:**		
32 Abbots Road	32 Abbots Road	**Mobile:**		
Broadmeadows	Broadmeadows	**Email:**	info@hd.com.au	
VIC	VIC	**Credit Limit:**	$6,000.00	
		Sales Rep:		
3047	3047	**Default Price List:**	Default Price List	

Name	Category	Active	Contact Name	Telephone	Balance
Peter Electronics		Yes	Megan Boucher	0391234567	$2,300.00

Delivery Address:	**Postal Address:**	**Fax:**		
9 Western Avenue	9 Western Avenue	**Mobile:**		
Brooklyn	Brooklyn	**Email:**	info@pe.com.au	
VIC	VIC	**Credit Limit:**	$3,000.00	
		Sales Rep:		
3012	3012	**Default Price List:**	Default Price List	

Name	Category	Active	Contact Name	Telephone	Balance
Sally's Warehouse		Yes	George Gordon	0394567890	$7,600.00

Delivery Address:	**Postal Address:**	**Fax:**		
12 Wood Street	12 Wood Street	**Mobile:**		
Essendon	Essendon	**Email:**	info@sw.com.au	
VIC	VIC	**Credit Limit:**	$10,000.00	
		Sales Rep:		
3040	3040	**Default Price List:**	Default Price List	

Name	Category	Active	Contact Name	Telephone	Balance
Surf Stores		Yes	Natalie Dunn	0393456789	$2,370.00

Delivery Address:	**Postal Address:**	**Fax:**		
54 Dundee Street	54 Dundee Street	**Mobile:**		
Deer Park	Deer Park	**Email:**	info@ss.com.au	
VIC	VIC	**Credit Limit:**	$3,000.00	
		Sales Rep:		
3023	3023	**Default Price List:**	Default Price List	

Name	Category	Active	Contact Name	Telephone	Balance
Thomson Clothings		Yes	Alston Leeson	0396789012	$0.00

Delivery Address:	**Postal Address:**	**Fax:**		
84 Spring Street	84 Spring Street	**Mobile:**		
Thomastown	Thomastown	**Email:**	info@thc.com.au	
VIC	VIC	**Credit Limit:**	$5,000.00	
		Sales Rep:		
3074	3074	**Default Price List:**	Default Price List	

Customer Listing Report

Richmond Papers Pty Ltd

	Date:	09/05/2016
	Page:	2/2

Name	Category	Active	Contact Name	Telephone	Balance
Tiffany Cakes		Yes	Anthony Robins	0398901234	$0.00

Delivery Address:	**Postal Address:**	**Fax:**		
36 High Road	36 High Road	**Mobile:**	
Williamstown	Williamstown	**Email:**	info@tc.com.au
VIC	VIC	**Credit Limit:**	$10,000.00
		Sales Rep:	
3016	3016	**Default Price List:**	Default Price List

Name	Category	Active	Contact Name	Telephone	Balance
Western Estate Agents		Yes	Ashley Champ	0392345678	$1,400.00

Delivery Address:	**Postal Address:**	**Fax:**		
362 High Street	362 High Street	**Mobile:**	
Sunshine	Sunshine	**Email:**	info@wea.com.au
VIC	VIC	**Credit Limit:**	$2,000.00
		Sales Rep:	
3029	3029	**Default Price List:**	Default Price List

Customer Transactions Report

Richmond Papers Pty Ltd

Customer:	All Customers
Category:	All Categories
Date Range:	01/04/2016 - 30/04/2016

Customer

Date	Reference	Transaction Type	Description	Debit	Credit	Balance
Globe Travels Pty Ltd						
Opening Balance as at: 01/04/2016				$ 0.00		
12/04/2016	INV0000003	Tax Invoice		$ 7,880.00		$ 7,880.00
20/04/2016	RCP0000003	Customer Receipt			$ 7,880.00	$ 0.00
Closing Balance as at: 30/04/2016				$ 0.00		
Movement for the period					$ 0.00	
Horizon Designs						
Opening Balance as at: 01/04/2016				$ 0.00		
05/04/2016	INV0000001	Tax Invoice		$ 5,235.00		$ 5,235.00
13/04/2016	RCP0000001	Customer Receipt			$ 5,235.00	$ 0.00
Closing Balance as at: 30/04/2016				$ 0.00		
Movement for the period					$ 0.00	
Peter Electronics						
Opening Balance as at: 01/04/2016				$ 0.00		
19/04/2016	INV0000005	Tax Invoice		$ 2,300.00		$ 2,300.00
Closing Balance as at: 30/04/2016				$ 2,300.00		
Movement for the period				$ 2,300.00		
Sally's Warehouse						
Opening Balance as at: 01/04/2016				$ 0.00		
21/04/2016	INV0000006	Tax Invoice		$ 7,750.00		$ 7,750.00
23/04/2016	CRN0000002	Credit Note			$ 150.00	$ 7,600.00
Closing Balance as at: 30/04/2016				$ 7,600.00		
Movement for the period				$ 7,600.00		
Surf Stores						
Opening Balance as at: 01/04/2016				$ 0.00		
27/04/2016	INV0000008	Tax Invoice		$ 2,370.00		$ 2,370.00
Closing Balance as at: 30/04/2016				$ 2,370.00		
Movement for the period				$ 2,370.00		
Thomson Clothings						
Opening Balance as at: 01/04/2016				$ 0.00		
10/04/2016	INV0000002	Tax Invoice		$ 3,700.00		$ 3,700.00
17/04/2016	CRN0000001	Credit Note			$ 700.00	$ 3,000.00
18/04/2016	RCP0000002	Customer Receipt			$ 3,000.00	$ 0.00
Closing Balance as at: 30/04/2016				$ 0.00		
Movement for the period					$ 0.00	
Tiffany Cakes						

Customer						
Date	Reference	Transaction Type	Description	Debit	Credit	Balance
Opening Balance as at: 01/04/2016				$ 0.00		
14/04/2016	INV0000004	Tax Invoice		$ 6,090.00		$ 6,090.00
25/04/2016	RCP0000004	Customer Receipt			$ 6,090.00	$ 0.00
Closing Balance as at: 30/04/2016				$ 0.00		
Movement for the period					$ 0.00	
Western Estate Agents						
Opening Balance as at: 01/04/2016				$ 0.00		
25/04/2016	INV0000007	Tax Invoice		$ 1,400.00		$ 1,400.00
Closing Balance as at: 30/04/2016				$ 1,400.00		
Movement for the period				$ 1,400.00		
Grand Total:				$ 13,670.00		

Purchases By Item Report

Richmond Papers Pty Ltd

Item:	All Items
Category:	All Categories
Date Range:	01/04/2016 - 30/04/2016

Date	Document No.	Supplier	Qty Purchased	Unit Price	Total Purchases
A3CP - A3 Copy Paper					
02/04/2016	SIV0000001	Gary Corporation	200	$ 22.73	$ 4,545.45
Total for A3CP - A3 Copy Paper			**200**	**$ 22.73**	**$ 4,545.45**
A4CP - A4 Copy Paper					
04/04/2016	SIV0000003	Ian & Co Pty Ltd	500	$ 7.27	$ 3,636.36
Total for A4CP - A4 Copy Paper			**500**	**$ 7.27**	**$ 3,636.36**
A5CP - A5 Copy Paper					
02/04/2016	SIV0000002	Smith & Baker	250	$ 7.27	$ 1,818.18
22/04/2016	RTN0000001	Smith & Baker	-20	$ 7.27	$ -145.45
Total for A5CP - A5 Copy Paper			**230**	**$ 7.27**	**$ 1,672.73**
COLO - Coloured Paper					
07/04/2016	SIV0000005	Mark & Tony	200	$ 12.73	$ 2,545.45
Total for COLO - Coloured Paper			**200**	**$ 12.73**	**$ 2,545.45**
EN01 - Envelopes Large					
09/04/2016	SIV0000006	East End Pty Ltd	200	$ 20.00	$ 4,000.00
Total for EN01 - Envelopes Large			**200**	**$ 20.00**	**$ 4,000.00**
RR18 - Register Rolls					
05/04/2016	SIV0000004	David & Sons	350	$ 34.55	$ 12,090.91
22/04/2016	RTN0000002	David & Sons	-25	$ 34.55	$ -863.64
Total for RR18 - Register Rolls			**325**	**$ 34.55**	**$ 11,227.27**
Grand Total			**1,655**		**$ 27,627.26**

Item Valuation Report

Richmond Papers Pty Ltd

Item: All Items
Category: All Categories
Date Range: 30/04/2016
Cost: Average Cost

Code	Description	Category	Active	On Hand	Cost	Value
A3CP	A3 Copy Paper		Yes	80	$ 22.73	$ 1,818.40
A4CP	A4 Copy Paper		Yes	90	$ 7.27	$ 654.30
A5CP	A5 Copy Paper		Yes	60	$ 7.27	$ 436.20
COLO	Coloured Paper		Yes	10	$ 12.73	$ 127.30
EN01	Envelopes Large		Yes	80	$ 20.00	$ 1,600.00
RR18	Register Rolls		Yes	55	$ 34.55	$ 1,900.25
Total:						**$ 6,536.45**

Banks and Credit Cards Transactions Report

Richmond Papers Pty Ltd

Bank Account:	All Bank Accounts
Category:	All Categories
Date Range:	01/04/2016 - 30/04/2016

Bank Account				Transaction	Account / Customer /			
Date	Payee	Description	Reference	Type	Supplier	Debit	Credit	Balance
Current Account								
Opening Balance as at: 01/04/2016						**$ 0.00**		
01/04/2016	Richmond Papers Pty Ltd	Capital Introduced	CR0001	Account Receipt	Owners Contribution	$ 25,000.00		$ 25,000.00
02/04/2016	Richmond Motors	Motor vehicle purchased	000001	Account Payment	Motor Vehicles - At Cost		$ 13,200.00	$ 11,800.00
02/04/2016	Richmond Real Estate	Rent	000002	Account Payment	Rent Paid		$ 1,100.00	$ 10,700.00
07/04/2016	Melbourne Insurance	Insurance Premium	000003	Account Payment	Insurance		$ 220.00	$ 10,480.00
13/04/2016			RCP0000001	Customer Receipt	Horizon Designs	$ 5,235.00		$ 15,715.00
18/04/2016			RCP0000002	Customer Receipt	Thomson Clothings	$ 3,000.00		$ 18,715.00
19/04/2016	Victoria Electricity	Electricity Bill	000004	Account Payment	Electricity & Water		$ 194.40	$ 18,520.60
20/04/2016			RCP0000003	Customer Receipt	Globe Travels Pty Ltd	$ 7,880.00		$ 26,400.60
21/04/2016	Australia Telecom	Telephone Bill	000005	Account Payment	Telephone & Internet		$ 215.84	$ 26,184.76
22/04/2016		000007	PAY0000001	Supplier Payment	Gary Corporation		$ 5,000.00	$ 21,184.76
25/04/2016			RCP0000004	Customer Receipt	Tiffany Cakes	$ 6,090.00		$ 27,274.76
26/04/2016	Melbourne Removals	Cleaning	000006	Account Payment	Cleaning		$ 55.00	$ 27,219.76
28/04/2016		000008	PAY0000002	Supplier Payment	Smith & Baker		$ 1,840.00	$ 25,379.76
30/04/2016	Bank of Richmond	Bank Charges	300416	Account Payment	Bank Charges		$ 10.00	$ 25,369.76
Closing Balance as at: 30/04/2016						**$ 25,369.76**		
Movement for the period						**$ 25,369.76**		
Grand Total:							**$ 25,369.76**	

Bank Reconciliation Report

Richmond Papers Pty Ltd

		Date:	09/05/2016
		Page:	1/1

Account Name: Current Account

Closing Balance As Per Bank Statement : $27,264.76

Less Outstanding Payments :

28/04/2016	PAY0000002	Supplier Payment	000008	$-1,840.00
26/04/2016	000006	Account Payment	Cleaning	$-55.00

                                                                                                          $-1,895.00

Plus Outstanding Receipts :

Reconciled Bank Balance		$25,369.76
Computer Bank Balance As At	30/04/2016	$25,369.76
Diff		$0.00

Journal Entries Report

Richmond Papers Pty Ltd

Date: 09/05/2016
Page: 1/1

Date	Description	Reference	Account	Debit	Credit
30/04/2016	Motor Vehicle Depreciation	300416	Depreciation	$100.00	
30/04/2016	Motor Vehicle Depreciation	300416	Tax Payable	$0.00	
30/04/2016	Motor Vehicle Depreciation	300416	Motor Vehicles - Accumulated Depreciation		$100.00
				$100.00	$100.00

Trial Balance Report

Richmond Papers Pty Ltd

Date Range: 01/07/2015 - 30/04/2016

Name	Category	Source	Debit	Credit
A3 Copy Paper	Sales	Sales/Purchases Account		$ 4,363.63
A4 Copy Paper	Sales	Sales/Purchases Account		$ 5,559.10
A5 Copy Paper	Sales	Sales/Purchases Account		$ 2,163.64
Coloured Paper	Sales	Sales/Purchases Account		$ 3,454.55
Envelopes Large	Sales	Sales/Purchases Account		$ 3,818.18
Register Rolls	Sales	Sales/Purchases Account		$ 13,254.54
A3 Copy Paper	Cost of Sales	Sales/Purchases Account	$ 4,545.45	
A4 Copy Paper	Cost of Sales	Sales/Purchases Account	$ 3,636.36	
A5 Copy Paper	Cost of Sales	Sales/Purchases Account	$ 1,672.73	
Coloured Paper	Cost of Sales	Sales/Purchases Account	$ 2,545.45	
Envelopes Large	Cost of Sales	Sales/Purchases Account	$ 4,000.00	
Register Rolls	Cost of Sales	Sales/Purchases Account	$ 11,227.27	
Bank Charges	Expenses	Account Balance	$ 10.00	
Cleaning	Expenses	Account Balance	$ 50.00	
Depreciation	Expenses	Account Balance	$ 100.00	
Electricity & Water	Expenses	Account Balance	$ 176.73	
Insurance	Expenses	Account Balance	$ 200.00	
Rent Paid	Expenses	Account Balance	$ 1,000.00	
Telephone & Internet	Expenses	Account Balance	$ 196.22	
Motor Vehicles - Accumulated Depreciation	Non-Current Assets	Account Balance		$ 100.00
Motor Vehicles - At Cost	Non-Current Assets	Account Balance	$ 12,000.00	
Current Account	Current Assets	Bank Account Balance	$ 25,369.76	
Trade Receivables	Current Assets	System Account	$ 13,670.00	
Tax Payable	Current Liabilities	System Account	$ 863.67	
Trade Payables	Current Liabilities	System Account		$ 23,550.00
Owners Contribution	Owners Equity	Account Balance		$ 25,000.00
			$ 81,263.64	$ 81,263.64
Net Profit/Loss After Tax				$ 3,253.43

Profit and Loss Report

Richmond Papers Pty Ltd

Date Range:	01/04/2016 - 30/04/2016
Cost of Sales:	Based on Purchases

	Apr 16
Sales	
A3 Copy Paper	4,364
A4 Copy Paper	5,559
A5 Copy Paper	2,164
Coloured Paper	3,455
Envelopes Large	3,818
Register Rolls	13,255
Total for Sales	**32,614**
Cost of Sales	
A3 Copy Paper	4,545
A4 Copy Paper	3,636
A5 Copy Paper	1,673
Coloured Paper	2,545
Envelopes Large	4,000
Register Rolls	11,227
Total for Cost of Sales	**27,627**
Gross Profit	**4,986**
Other Income	
Total for Other Income	**0**
Expenses	
Bank Charges	10
Cleaning	50
Depreciation	100
Electricity & Water	177
Insurance	200
Rent Paid	1,000
Telephone & Internet	196
Total for Expenses	**1,733**
Net Profit/Loss Before Tax	**3,253**
Income Tax	0
Net Profit/Loss After Tax	**3,253**

Date Printed: 09/05/2016   Page 1 of 1

Balance Sheet Report

Richmond Papers Pty Ltd

Run At Date: 30/04/2016

Assets	
Non-Current Assets	
Motor Vehicles - Accumulated Depreciation	$ -100.00
Motor Vehicles - At Cost	$ 12,000.00
Total Non-Current Assets	$ 11,900.00
Current Assets	
Current Account	$ 25,369.76
Tax Payable	$ 863.67
Trade Receivables	$ 13,670.00
Total Current Assets	$ 39,903.43
Total Assets	$ 51,803.43
Equity and Liabilities	
Owners Equity	
Profit and Loss (This Year)	$ 3,253.43
Owners Contribution	$ 25,000.00
Total Owners Equity	$ 28,253.43
Non-Current Liabilities	
Total Non-Current Liabilities	$ 0.00
Current Liabilities	
Trade Payables	$ 23,550.00
Total Current Liabilities	$ 23,550.00
Total Equity and Liabilities	$ 51,803.43

Date Printed. 09/05/2016   Page 1 of 1

www.ingramcontent.com/pod-product-compliance
Lightning Source LLC
Chambersburg PA
CBHW060514060326
40689CB00020B/4747